Riley the Robot
An Input/Output Machine

Kathleen L. Stone

Enjoy these other books by Mrs. Stone

Penguin Place Value
A Math Adventure

Number Line Fun
Solving Number Mysteries

Mason the Magician
Hundreds Chart Addition

Copyright © 2014 Kathleen L. Stone

All rights reserved.

ISBN-10: 1499248814
ISBN-13: 978-1499248814

Dedication

What a gift to be able to spend my days teaching. I've learned so much from my students and am so happy they are a part of my life … a part of my heart.

Riley the Robot

Is quite a machine.

She's the best mathematician

You ever have seen.

Guess my rule

Input

Her favorite game
Is called "Guess My Rule."
You can play it at home,
In your car, or at school.

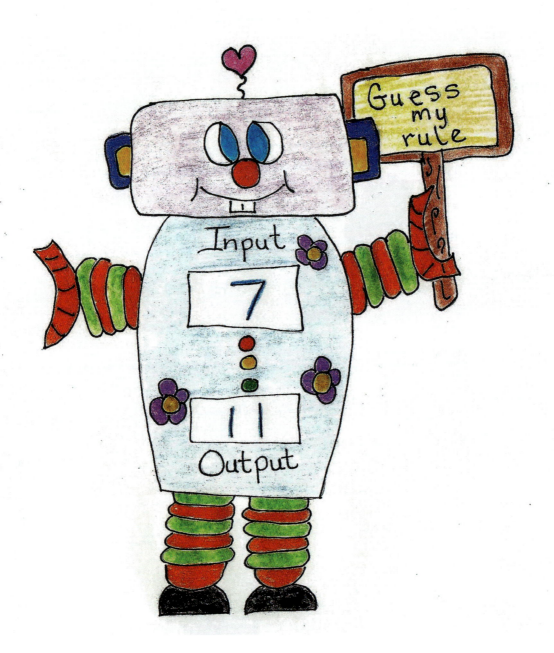

She puts in a number.

Soon another pops out.

Your job is to figure out

How that all came about.

It's really not hard

So don't look so blue.

It really is easy.

She'll give you a clue.

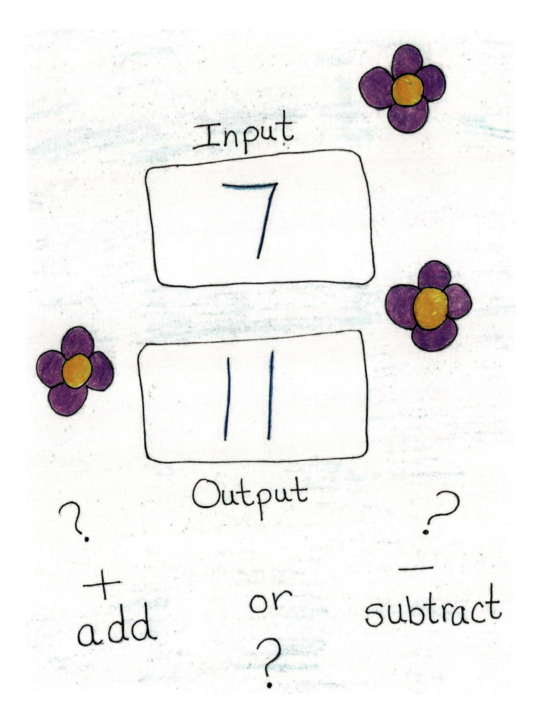

What would you do

If you started with *seven*?

Would you add or subtract

To end up with *eleven*?

Input
7

8, 9, 10, 11

+4

+1 +1 +1 +1
7 8 9 10 11

Let's try counting on …

Eight, nine, ten, eleven.

That really was easy!

You'd add *four* to that *seven*.

Okay, here's another

Riley thinks you'll do great.

She puts in a *six*

And out pops an *eight*.

If you started with *six*

What would you do

To end up with *eight*?

That's right! You'd add *two*!

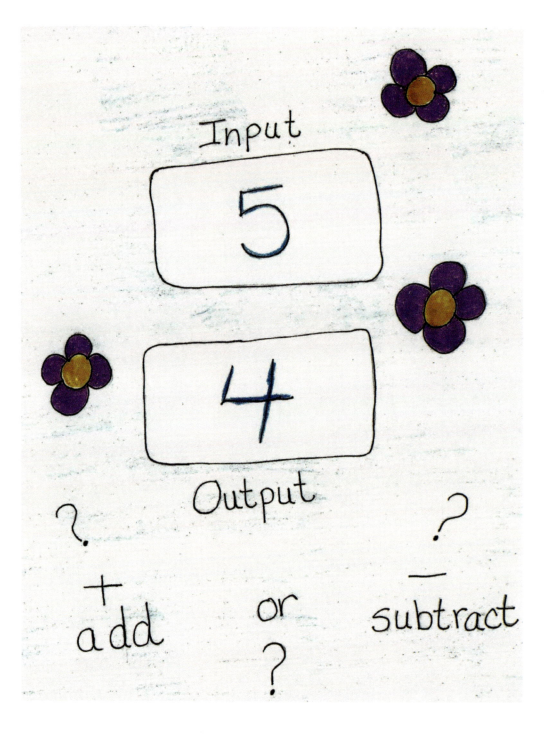

Riley has a new number.

Will you try just one more?

She puts in a *five*.

Out pops a *four!*

This problem's a bit tricky.

But it's still lots of fun.

To end up with *four*

You'd just take away *one*.

Now that you know

How to play Riley's game

Maybe someday you'll be

In the *Mathematician's Hall of Fame*

Algebraic Concepts: Input/Output (*Functions*)

Riley the Robot provides children practice with the higher level algebraic concept of *Input/Output* or *Functions*. A number goes **in,** Riley does something to it, and another number comes **out**. Sometimes this skill is taught as *missing addends and minuends*.

Children should be given plenty of opportunities to figure out the "rule" for various problems:

Human Input/Output Machine

- ♥ Place a large screen or box in the front of the room (I use my *Pocket Chart*).
- ♥ Give one child the numeral "3" and another child the numeral "10."
- ♥ Have the "input" child (#3) stand beside the screen (showing the class their number) and the "output" child (#10) stand behind the screen.
- ♥ The "input" child steps behind the screen as the "output" child steps out.
- ♥ Have the class identify the "rule" (in this case it is "+7").

Once children have a grasp of this concept they'll be ready to move on to more abstract problems:

What is the rule for this data table?

Input	Output
4	7
11	14
6	9
20	23
78	81

    A. Add 4
    B. Subtract 4
    C. Add 3

Fill in the missing numbers on this data table.
What is the rule?

Input	Output
1	11
5	
	20
27	
35	45

Rule _____

Made in the USA
San Bernardino, CA
20 August 2014